The MISEDUCATION of the Negro in the 21st Century – Middle School Student Workbook

Who Lives Like This?! Publishing LLC
www.nerdyouthservices.org

ISBN: 978-1-970680-09-6 (Paperback)

Cover design and interior layout by
Who Lives Like This?! Publishing LLC Design Team

Printed in the United States of America

First Edition — 2025

Dedication

This work is dedicated to every young mind determined to break free from the chains of miseducation. To the students who question, the teachers who empower, and the ancestors whose sacrifices paved the road we walk today.

May this guide serve as a light, a weapon, and a foundation.
Never forget — you were born to lead, not follow.
The world is your classroom. The truth is your legacy.

- Cedric A. Washington
Author. Educator. Revolutionary.

THE MISEDUCATION OF THE NEGRO IN THE 21ST CENTURY

MIDDLE SCHOOL STUDENT WORKBOOK (GRADES 6–8)

Teach Like Ced Series
Knowledge of S.E.L.F. (Social Empowerment Learning Framework)
By **Cedric A. Washington**

HOW TO USE THIS WORKBOOK (STUDENT DIRECTIONS)

For each chapter you will complete:

- **Step 1: Vocabulary (from the reading)**
- **Step 2: Close Reading**
- **Step 3: Constructed Response (CER)**
- **Step 4: Extended Writing**
- **Step 5: Discussion Prep**
- **Step 6: Knowledge of SELF Connection**
- **Step 7: Exit Ticket**

Non-negotiable rule: All answers must come **from the text**.

PREFACE — WORKBOOK PAGES

Step 1 — Vocabulary (from the Preface)

Write the meaning using the Preface context (your own words, based on the text).

1. pedagogy: _____
2. ramifications: _____
3. state standards: _____
4. mainstream: _____
5. curriculums: _____
6. cultural competency: _____

7. urban education: _____

8. equivalent: _____

9. Soul Food: _____

10. scraps: _____

11. lack of resources: _____

12. undervalued: _____

13. institutionalized: _____

14. constraints: _____

15. compliant: _____

16. rules and regulations: _____

17. demerit/merit system: _____

18. data driven: _____

19. reprimand: _____

20. redirect: _____

21. insubordinate: _____

22. "bucking the system": _____

23. pop-up shop schools: _____

24. ideologies: _____

25. perpetuate: _____

26. courageous: _____

27. shackles: _____

28. intellectual jargon: _____

29. empty rhetoric: _____

30. biased: _____

31. crime: _____

32. destiny: _____

33. Education: _____

34. Knowledge: _____

35. slavery: _____

36. culture: _____

37. cultivate: _____

38. control: _____

39. mentoring: _____

40. relate: _____

Step 2 — Close Reading (Preface)

Answer using the Preface only.

1. What does the author say education can do to the pedagogy of the best teachers?

---

2. Why does the author compare urban education to "Soul Food"?

_____

_____

3. What does the author describe about "models" versus "listening to the expert"?

_____

_____

4. Explain the author's discipline example: "Tuck your shirt in… and we both continue our day." What point is he making?

_____

_____

5. What is the author calling "a crime" in the Preface?

_____

_____

6. According to the author, what is the difference between education and knowledge?

_____

_____

_____

Step 3 — Constructed Response (CER) — Preface

Prompt: Explain why the author says, "I am a free man," and what he means by freedom in education.

C (Claim): _____

E (Evidence — quote or paraphrase from Preface):

_____

_____

R (Reasoning): _____

_____

_____

Step 4 — Extended Writing — Preface

Prompt: The author argues that miseducation is harming communities. Write one well-organized paragraph explaining his message, using at least **two** pieces of evidence from the Preface.

Paragraph:

_____
_____
_____
_____
_____
_____

Step 5 — Discussion Prep — Preface

Choose **one** quote from the Preface and explain what it means.

Quote: "_____"

Meaning:

_____
_____
_____

Step 6 — Knowledge of SELF Connection (Preface)

Complete using Preface language.

SELF Conscience: What is the author asking people to become aware of?

_____

Social Conscience: What does he call the community to do together?

_____
_____

Step 7 — Exit Ticket — Preface

In one sentence, write the main message of the Preface.

_____
_____

CHAPTER 1 — PRIVILEGE (WORKBOOK PAGES)

Step 1 — Vocabulary (from Chapter 1)

Use Chapter 1 context.

1. deficit: _____
2. disproportionality: _____
3. plague: _____
4. inner cities: _____
5. pop-up shop institutions: _____
6. charter schools: _____
7. public school systems: _____
8. ideologies: _____
9. rhetoric: _____
10. qualifications: _____
11. certification status: _____
12. non-traditional grading scales: _____
13. influx: _____
14. mainstream standards: _____
15. benchmarks: _____
16. parameters: _____
17. privilege: _____
18. constitutional layout: _____
19. liberty and justice for all: _____
20. enslaved: _____
21. publicized: _____
22. psychologically enslaved: _____
23. propaganda: _____
24. superiority: _____
25. inferiority: _____
26. systematic structure: _____
27. dissipated: _____
28. threatened: _____
29. abused: _____
30. oppressed: _____
31. housing segregation: _____
32. wealth disparities: _____
33. stable sense of knowledge of self: _____

Step 2 — Close Reading (Chapter 1)

1. What does the author say happened in Black America "dating back to the 1980s"?

_____

2. Why does the author title the chapter "Privilege"?

_____

3. According to the author, what did Woodson mean by "transform the Negroes, not develop them"?

_____

4. List two ways the author describes systems keeping people under a "glass ceiling."

_____

_____

5. What does the author say white liberal teachers must do?

_____

_____

Step 3 — Constructed Response (CER) — Chapter 1

Prompt: Explain how privilege affects education in Chapter 1.

C: _____

E: _____

R: _____

Step 4 — Extended Writing — Chapter 1

Prompt: The author argues that accurate history and culture must be taught. Write a paragraph explaining why, using two text-based details.

_____

_____

_____

_____

Step 5 — Discussion Prep — Chapter 1

Respond to this statement using the chapter:
"It is not noble… when the system is still being perpetuated to our demise."

Your response:

_____

_____

Step 6 — Knowledge of SELF Connection — Chapter 1

SELF Conscience: What does the author say is missing without knowledge of self?

_____

Social Conscience: What role does the author give "allies" in change?

_____

_____

Step 7 — Exit Ticket — Chapter 1

One sentence: What is privilege in this chapter?

_____

_____

CHAPTER 2 — FIGUREHEAD (WORKBOOK PAGES)

Step 1 — Vocabulary (from Chapter 2)

1. figurehead: _____
2. nominal leader: _____
3. enslaved mind: _____
4. defend the system: _____
5. procession: _____
6. admiration: _____
7. implement: _____
8. badge of honor: _____
9. muzzle: _____

10. authorities: _____

11. dysfunctionality: _____

12. exploit: _____

13. "sweat the small stuff": _____

14. school to prison pipeline: _____

15. tyrannical: _____

16. doctrine: _____

17. Hunger Games: _____

18. desegregation: _____

19. house negro: _____

20. field negro: _____

21. conscience: _____

22. hamster wheel: _____

Step 2 — Close Reading (Chapter 2)

1. Define figurehead using the chapter's definition.

_____

2. What is the "danger" of figurehead leadership in schools?

_____

3. What does the author say black principals must acknowledge?

_____

4. How does the text connect discipline policies to the school-to-prison pipeline?

_____

Step 3 — Constructed Response (CER) — Chapter 2

Prompt: Explain why the author compares figurehead leadership to "house negro."

C: _____

E: _____

R: _____

Step 4 — Extended Writing — Chapter 2

Prompt: Write a paragraph explaining what "true leadership" requires in this chapter.

_____
_____
_____

Step 5 — Discussion Prep — Chapter 2

Choose one "figurehead-ism" quote from the opening lines and explain what it reveals.

Quote: "_____"
Meaning: _____

Step 6 — Knowledge of SELF Connection — Chapter 2

SELF Governing: What does leadership require besides "shaking and nodding"?

_____
_____

Step 7 — Exit Ticket — Chapter 2

One sentence: What is a figurehead?

_____
_____

CHAPTER 3 — KNOWLEDGE VS. EDUCATION (WORKBOOK PAGES)

Step 1 — Vocabulary (from Chapter 3)

1. systematic instruction: _____
2. oppressor: _____
3. miseducation: _____
4. SEL (Social Emotional Learning): _____
5. five core competencies: _____
6. self-awareness: _____

7. resilience: _____
8. internal cues: _____
9. blind spots: _____
10. lenses: _____
11. identity: _____
12. distinguishing character: _____
13. psychological identification: _____
14. preconceived notion: _____
15. over generalizing: _____
16. jaded: _____
17. cultural characteristics: _____
18. cognitive dissonance: _____
19. inconsistent thoughts: _____
20. melanin: _____
21. complexion: _____
22. connotation: _____
23. intentional: _____
24. wisdom: _____

Step 2 — Close Reading (Chapter 3)

1. What is the author's main difference between knowledge and education?

2. Why does the author say the CASEL model is "shallow" for the so-called African American youth?

3. What does the author say identity is, using the chapter's definition?

4. Explain the melanin/skin tone chart lesson. What is the purpose?

Step 3 — Constructed Response (CER) — Chapter 3

Prompt: Explain how "identity" connects to self-awareness in this chapter.

C: _____

E: _____

R: _____

Step 4 — Extended Writing — Chapter 3

Prompt: Write a paragraph explaining why the author calls controlled learning "slavery."

_____

_____

_____

Step 5 — Discussion Prep — Chapter 3

Respond: "Can you be educated and still be clueless? That is called slavery."

Your response using evidence:

_____

_____

Step 6 — Knowledge of SELF Connection — Chapter 3

SELF Conscience: What does the author build in students through "Love Yourself (The Skin You're In)"?

_____

_____

Step 7 — Exit Ticket — Chapter 3

One sentence: What is cognitive dissonance in this chapter?

_____

_____

CHAPTER 4 — CULTURE = INTELLIGENCE = BEHAVIOR (WORKBOOK PAGES)

Step 1 — Vocabulary (from Chapter 4)

1. phenomenon: _____
2. correct and re-correct: _____
3. substantial original historical base: _____
4. multiplicity: _____
5. phenomena of illusion: _____
6. orbit: _____
7. bourgeoisies: _____
8. authenticity: _____
9. audacity: _____
10. rearing: _____
11. idiosyncrasies: _____
12. paranoia: _____
13. disproportionality: _____
14. insecurities: _____
15. standard of beauty: _____
16. neutralized: _____
17. product of your environment: _____

Step 2 — Close Reading (Chapter 4)

1. What does the author mean by culture shaping intelligence and behavior?

2. How does the author use the Willie Lynch theory to explain cultural conditioning?

3. Give one modern example from the chapter showing how past trauma shows today.

4. Explain how Trading Places supports the chapter's point.

Step 3 — Constructed Response (CER) — Chapter 4

Prompt: Explain how the mind "corrects and re-corrects" once exposed to historical base.

C: _____
E: _____
R: _____

Step 4 — Extended Writing — Chapter 4

Prompt: Write a paragraph explaining "product of your environment" using the chapter's details.

_____

_____

Step 5 — Discussion Prep — Chapter 4

Respond using the text: Why does culture have to be "controlled" for destiny to change?

_____

_____

Step 6 — Knowledge of SELF Connection — Chapter 4

SELF Conscience: What does the author say is needed to reconnect to origin?

_____

_____

Step 7 — Exit Ticket — Chapter 4

One sentence: Define "Culture = Intelligence = Behavior."

_____

_____

CHAPTER 5 — PARENTS AND THE ENVIRONMENT (WORKBOOK PAGES)

(Directly matches your Chapter 5 TE steps)

Step 1 — Vocabulary (from Chapter 5)

1. intelligence: _____

2. environment: _____
3. trauma: _____
4. psychological effect: _____
5. dominant species: _____
6. authority: _____
7. absenteeism: _____
8. role models: _____
9. mentoring: _____
10. vulgarity: _____
11. disrespect: _____
12. accountability: _____
13. redirecting: _____
14. delusional: _____
15. code of ethics: _____
16. normalcy: _____
17. defense mechanism: _____
18. agendas: _____
19. common denominator: _____
20. product: _____

Step 2 — Close Reading (Chapter 5)

1. What does the author mean when he asks, "But what if you really do not know better?"

2. How does the chapter connect Willie Lynch to parenting and environment?

3. What does the author say happens when the man is removed from the home?

4. Identify two school elements that contribute to the miseducation described.

Step 3 — Constructed Response (CER) — Chapter 5

Prompt: Explain how environment shapes behavior in this chapter.

C: _____

E: _____

R: _____

Step 4 — Extended Writing — Chapter 5

Prompt: Write a paragraph explaining why collective organization is necessary, using evidence.

Step 5 — Discussion Prep — Chapter 5

Respond using text: "Misinformed adults raise misinformed children…"

Step 6 — Knowledge of SELF Connection — Chapter 5

Social Conscience: What does the author call parents and community to take ownership of?

Step 7 — Exit Ticket — Chapter 5

One sentence: What is the author's demand in this chapter?

CHAPTER 6 — HIP-HOP (WORKBOOK PAGES)

(Correlated to your Chapter 6 TE)

Step 1 — Vocabulary (from Chapter 6)

Hip-Hop • boogie down Bronx • black CNN • phenomenon • mainstream • exploitation • contract • jargon • master • slave • intellectual property • privilege • House Negro • Field Negro • culture • glorified • conscience • narrative • cognitive dissonance • endearment • connotation • colonized • origin

Write meanings using the chapter context:

1. Hip-Hop: _____
2. master: _____
3. slave: _____
4. intellectual property: _____
5. exploitation: _____
6. conscience: _____
7. narrative: _____
8. cognitive dissonance: _____

Step 2 — Close Reading (Chapter 6)

1. What does the author say Hip-Hop became globally since 2017?

_____

2. Why does the author discuss "master and slave" in music contracts?

_____

3. How does the House Negro vs. Field Negro analogy apply to artists?

_____

4. What is the author's warning about the word "nigger/nigga"?

_____

Step 3 — Constructed Response (CER) — Chapter 6

Prompt: Explain why the author says, "Hip-Hop was created to tell a story not sell a story."

C: _____
E: _____
R: _____

Step 4 — Extended Writing — Chapter 6

Prompt: Argue whether Hip-Hop is helping or harming culture today, using only Chapter 6 evidence.

_____

Step 5 — Discussion Prep — Chapter 6

Answer: "Is Hip-Hop teaching or selling culture?" (Use text)

Step 6 — Knowledge of SELF Connection — Chapter 6

SELF Conscience: What identity issue does the author connect to Hip-Hop language?

Step 7 — Exit Ticket — Chapter 6

One sentence: What does the author mean by "Wake yo' ass up!"

CHAPTER 7 — POLITICS (WORKBOOK PAGES)

(Correlated to your Chapter 7 TE)

Step 1 — Vocabulary (from Chapter 7)

pledge • republic • indivisible • Jim Crow • voting act • injustices • disproportionalities • Democrats • Republicans • agenda • Wakanda • patronize • escalator style • hamster wheel • socio-economic • figurative glass ceiling • black dollar • organize • construct • independence

Define using context:

1. agenda: _____
2. hamster wheel: _____
3. black dollar: _____
4. figurative glass ceiling: _____

Step 2 — Close Reading (Chapter 7)

1. Why does the author repeat "opportunities, employment, and justice"?

---

2. What does the chapter say about party loyalty and outcomes?

3. What does the author propose as a solution?

Step 3 — Constructed Response (CER) — Chapter 7

Prompt: Explain why voting alone is not enough in this chapter.

C: _____

E: _____

R: _____

Step 4 — Extended Writing — Chapter 7

Prompt: Write a paragraph explaining economic power as political power, using evidence.

Step 5 — Discussion Prep — Chapter 7

Respond: "No Democrat or Republican can help us with that."

Step 6 — Knowledge of SELF Connection — Chapter 7

SELF Governing: What does the author say people must do "on our own"?

Step 7 — Exit Ticket — Chapter 7

One sentence: What is the "black agenda" in the author's framing?

CHAPTER 8 — THE BLACK CHURCH (WORKBOOK PAGES)

Step 1 — Vocabulary (from Chapter 8)

manipulation • worship • doctrine • denominations • oppressor • miseducation • cognitive dissonance • entertainment • sustenance • Ephesians 6:5–6 • COINTELPRO • 501(c)(3) • amendment • prohibition • communal effort • individualistic prosperity • illusion • revelation

Define using context:

1. doctrine: _____
2. communal effort: _____
3. illusion: _____
4. prohibition: _____
5. miseducation: _____

Step 2 — Close Reading (Chapter 8)

1. How does the author describe the Black church in the 21st Century?

_____

2. Why does the author reference Ephesians 6:5–6?

_____

3. What political limitation does the chapter cite for churches, and why does it matter?

_____

4. What does the author say the Black church has "forgotten"?

_____

Step 3 — Constructed Response (CER) — Chapter 8

Prompt: Explain why the author calls the Black church the "biggest culprit."

C: _____

E: _____

R: _____

Step 4 — Extended Writing — Chapter 8

Prompt: Write a paragraph explaining faith vs. works using only Chapter 8 logic and evidence.

Step 5 — Discussion Prep — Chapter 8

Answer: "Can faith liberate people if history is ignored?" (Use the chapter.)

Step 6 — Knowledge of SELF Connection — Chapter 8

SELF Conscience: What truth does the author want the community to face?

Step 7 — Exit Ticket — Chapter 8

One sentence: What is the main message of Chapter 8?

CHAPTER 9 — REVELATION (FOUR HUNDRED YEARS ARE UP) (WORKBOOK PAGES)

(Correlated to your Chapter 9 TE)

Step 1 — Vocabulary (from Chapter 9)

miseducation • revelation • doctrine • interpretation • Old Testament • New Testament • historically accurate • transformations • King James Bible • curse • Deuteronomy 28 • reparations • pandemic • uprising • chosen people • destiny • awakening • culture • intelligence • behavior

Define using context:

1. miseducation: _____
2. revelation: _____
3. interpretation: _____

4. curse: _____

5. reparations: _____

Step 2 — Close Reading (Chapter 9)

1. What definition of miseducation does the author use?

_____

2. What does the author say mainstream education teaches as the start of Black history?

_____

3. Why does the author connect COVID-19 and George Floyd to revelation?

_____

4. What does "four hundred years are up" mean in the chapter's message?

_____

Step 3 — Constructed Response (CER) — Chapter 9

Prompt: Explain what revelation is and why it matters now, using only Chapter 9.

C: _____

E: _____

R: _____

Step 4 — Extended Writing — Chapter 9

Prompt: Write a paragraph summarizing the author's full call to action in Chapter 9.

_____

Step 5 — Discussion Prep — Chapter 9

Answer: "What happens when people learn the truth about who they are?"

_____

Step 6 — Knowledge of SELF Connection — Chapter 9

Aspirations: What future vision does the author describe for NERD Youth Services and Project UPLIFT?

Step 7 — Exit Ticket — Chapter 9

One sentence: What is the "revelation" in this chapter?

FINAL SECTION — CULMINATING PERFORMANCE TASK (TEXT-DERIVED)

Culminating Task (Grades 6–8)

Prompt: Using evidence from multiple chapters, explain how the author connects:
Culture → Intelligence → Behavior → Education → Destiny

Requirements:

- Use **at least 3 chapters**
- Use **text-based evidence**
- Use **vocabulary from the text**

Planning:

- Chapters used: _____
- Evidence 1: _____
- Evidence 2: _____
- Evidence 3: _____

Final Response (write on separate paper or lined pages provided by teacher).

www.ingramcontent.com/pod-product-compliance
Lightning Source LLC
Chambersburg PA
CBHW052118020426

42335CB00021B/2820